Welcome to
INDIA

Gareth Stevens Publishing
MILWAUKEE

Written by
FIONA CONBOY/SUNANDINI ARORA LAL

Designed by
LYNN CHIN NYUK LING

Picture research by
SUSAN JANE MANUEL

First published in North America in 2000 by
Gareth Stevens Publishing
1555 North RiverCenter Drive, Suite 201
Milwaukee, Wisconsin 53212 USA

For a free color catalog describing
Gareth Stevens' list of high-quality books
and multimedia programs, call
1-800-542-2595 (USA) or
1-800-461-9120 (CANADA).
Gareth Stevens Publishing's
Fax: (414) 225-0377.

© **TIMES EDITIONS PTE LTD 2000**
Originated and designed by
Times Editions Pte Ltd
Times Centre, 1 New Industrial Road
Singapore 536196
http://www.timesone.com.sg/te

Library of Congress Cataloging-in-Publication Data
available upon request from the publisher.
Fax: (414) 225-0377 for the attention of the
Publishing Records Department.

ISBN 0-8368-2497-0

Printed in Malaysia

1 2 3 4 5 6 7 8 9 04 03 02 01 00

PICTURE CREDITS
Bes Stock: 21
Susanna Burton: 26
Joginder Chawla: 7, 10, 14 (both), 15 (top),
    16, 20, 22, 23 (top), 25, 29, 34, 40, 41
Sylvia Cordaiy Photo Library: 18 (bottom), 19,
    30, 35
Fotomedia: cover, 1, 6, 9 (top), 17, 27,
    33 (both), 37, 39
The Hutchison Library: 9 (bottom), 28
Illustrated London News Picture Library: 12,
    15 (bottom)
Bjorn Kingwall: 23
Christine Osborne Pictures: 2, 3 (center), 5,
    8, 11
Liba Taylor Photography: 3 (bottom), 24, 31
Trip Photographic Library: 3 (top), 13,
    18 (top), 32, 36, 38, 43, 45

Digital Scanning by Superskill Graphics Pte Ltd

Contents

Words that appear in the glossary are printed in **boldface** type the first time they occur in the text.

Welcome to India!

India's history goes back more than five thousand years. Today, India is a country with seventeen official languages, a variety of races and religions, breathtaking scenery, and magnificent architecture. Let's explore the seventh largest country in the world and learn all about the people of India!

Opposite: Bombay Harbor's Gateway of India is a well-known **landmark**. Bombay is now called Mumbai.

Below: India's cities are greatly **overpopulated**, causing daily traffic jams. A scooter is a great way to get around!

The Flag of India

The Indian flag consists of orange, white, and green bands. The color orange stands for courage, white for peace, and green for fertility. A Buddhist emblem called a ***dharma chakra*** (DHAR-mah CHAK-rah) lies in the center.

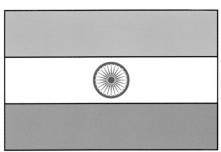

The Land

India borders China, Nepal, and Bhutan to the north, Pakistan to the west, and Bangladesh to the east. The Indian landscape varies from region to region.

India boasts many great mountain ranges, including the Vindhya Range, which divides northern and southern India. The Himalayan mountain range in northern India consists of some of the highest peaks in the world.

Below:
The Himalayan mountain range stretches over a distance of 1,500 miles (2,414 kilometers). It has some of the world's tallest peaks, including Mount Everest at 29,030 feet (8,848 meters).

Three major rivers flow through India. The Ganges is known as the holiest of rivers. It flows from the Himalayan mountains to Bangladesh. The Indus flows into Pakistan from the north, and the Brahmaputra runs across northeastern India from Tibet to Bangladesh.

The Thar Desert, India's driest region, extends across northern and northwestern Rajasthan.

Above: Many people travel far to bathe in the Ganges River, believing that its waters possess healing properties.

Climate

India has three main seasons — summer from March to May, the rainy season from June to September, and winter from October to February. India's size and variety of terrain — ranging from snowcapped peaks to desert plains — produce extreme weather patterns. Mountainous regions in the north experience the coldest temperatures, while temperatures average about 86° Fahrenheit (30° Celsius) in the south.

Above: The Thar Desert in Rajasthan receives only about 4 inches (102 millimeters) of rainfall per year.

Plants and Animals

India supports approximately 45,000 plant species, some of which are not found anywhere else in the world.

India's most well-known animal is the elephant. Other common animals include the bison, buffalo, black buck, rhinoceros, and monkey.

Above: These rare orchids grow in the eastern Himalayas.

Left: Elephants play an important part in religious and royal ceremonies in India.

History

Indus Valley Civilization

Not much is known about India's earliest inhabitants, who lived more than 200,000 years ago! **Archaeologists** have found evidence of the Indus Valley Civilization, a society that lasted from 2500 to 1700 B.C. In about 1500 B.C., a group called the Indo-Aryans arrived in India from Iran.

Above: Buddhism came to India in the third century B.C. This lion-topped pillar, decorated with symbols of Buddhist beliefs, is the emblem of the Indian government.

The Greeks and the Mauryans

In 326 B.C., Greek ruler Alexander the Great invaded India, introducing Western ideas. When he died, King Chandragupta from the Maurya **dynasty** took control of the Greek settlements. King Chandragupta became ruler of India, creating a single empire. After the collapse of the Mauryan Empire, India was divided once more. Many dynasties reigned, including the Sungas, Karvas, and Guptas.

The Mughal Empire

In 1524, Muslim king Babur invaded India from Central Asia and established the Mughal Empire. Under Babur's rule, India became a powerful nation once more. The Mughal Empire collapsed during the eighteenth century. By that time, another empire — the British — had entered India. The British, along with along with the French, Dutch, and Portuguese, set up trading posts.

Below: This is the site of the first Portuguese landing on the eastern coast of Kerala in 1498.

The British Empire

The British traded as the East India Company (EIC), extending control over the Mughal Empire. In 1818, India became part of the British Empire.

In 1857, a rebellion of Hindu and Muslim soldiers against the British nearly brought down the Empire. The Mughal king was **exiled**, and power was transferred from the EIC to the British Crown. India became a British colony, and a period of growth and development followed.

Left: The Indian revolt lasted from 1857 to 1859. The Indians refer to it as the First War of Independence; the British call it the Indian **Mutiny**.

The Fight for Independence

By the late 1800s, many Indians wanted independence from Britain. In 1885, Indian **nationalists** formed a political party called the Indian National Congress. One of its leaders, Mohandas Karamchand Gandhi, led peaceful **strikes** throughout India, fighting for independence and peace between Hindus and Muslims. Gandhi became known as the "Father of the Nation."

Above: The British helped build railroads and modern industries in India. By the end of the nineteenth century, however, the Indians wanted control of their country again.

India Today

India gained independence from the British in 1947, with Jawaharlal Nehru as prime minister. The Muslims, however, wanted a separate state, so the country of Pakistan was born. Millions of people died in the violence that broke out between the two countries.

In 1950, India became a **democratic** republic. Although the Indian National Congress remained powerful during the post-independence years, other political parties also grew in popularity.

Above: Yugoslav-born Mother Teresa of Calcutta founded the Missionaries of Charity to care for the poor in India.

Below: Thousands of Muslims left India for Pakistan when the two countries were divided.

Akbar (1542–1605)

Akbar, grandson of King Babur, was the greatest of the Mughal kings. He encouraged harmony between Muslims and Hindus and supported the arts.

Subhas Chandra Bose (1897–1945)

A committed nationalist, Bose launched the Indian National Army (INA) to free India from British rule during World War II (1939–1945). The INA was defeated, and Bose died shortly after the war.

Subhas Chandra Bose

Lord Louis Mountbatten (1900–1979)

Mountbatten supervised the transfer of power from Britain to India in 1947. After India gained independence, he became governor general of India.

Lord Louis Mountbatten

Government and the Economy

Government

The prime minister heads the Indian government, or Central Cabinet. India's head of state, the president, is elected by cabinet members. The parliament consists of the Lok Sabha (House of the People) and the Rajya Sabha (Council of States).

Below: New Delhi, home of Parliament House, is India's capital city.

Left: The Supreme Court in New Delhi can rule on new laws passed by the government.

States

India is divided into twenty-five states, each with its own governor, members of parliament, and lawmakers. The Indian people and local organizations elect the members of state parliaments.

People follow many different religions in India — Hinduism, Islam, Buddhism, Christianity — so the government has set up different laws to meet all of the people's needs.

Economy

India has a mixed economy of state-owned companies and private businesses. Since the 1990s, more and more foreign companies have started operations in India.

Above: India produces, consumes, and exports more black tea than any other country in the world.

Agriculture

About 70 percent of the Indian population works on the land. India exports tea and spices throughout the world. Other crops grown in India include rice, coffee, and cotton.

Left: Many Indian farms still use old-fashioned methods to plant and harvest crops.

Industry

India has a successful structure of factories and businesses. It is one of the world's leading producers of iron ore and coal. Its electrical, mechanical, and transportation industries also thrive.

Transportation

Three state-run Indian airlines provide local and international flights. With more than 1.7 million employees, Indian Railways is one of the world's biggest employers.

Above: The Indian railroad network was built by the British in the nineteenth century.

People and Lifestyle

The majority of Indian people descend from the Dravidians, the early inhabitants of the land. Other ethnic groups descend from the many peoples who settled in India from Central Asia, Arabia, and Greece. The people of northern India tend to have fair skin. People of Mongolian descent possess Asian features and live mainly in northeastern India.

Below: The Bhil tribe of western India celebrates a wedding.

Left: Young Indian girls dress in Western fashions and *salwarkameez* (sulh-WAHR-kuh-MEEZ), the outfits worn by the two girls on the left.

Each state and ethnic group has a distinct dress. People in the northern states wear woolen tops with cotton trousers. You can tell where a woman is from by the style in which she wears her **sari**.

Hindu women wear a ***bindi*** (BIN-dee) on their foreheads. It used to indicate marriage, but today, unmarried women wear bindi, too.

Family Life

In India, the family unit is very strong. It is common for three generations to live together under one roof. Traditionally, the father heads the household and has authority over most matters, including the children's upbringing. The mother manages the household and cares for the children. Today, however, as more women go out to work, this structure of family life is changing.

Above: Family ties are important in Hindu society.

Opposite: A Tamil Hindu bride and bridegroom take their marriage vows. The Tamils live mainly in southern India.

Marriage

The Indian people celebrate weddings enthusiastically. Friends and relatives might travel great distances to join in the festivities.

Some traditional families favor arranged marriages, and couples are matched according to their religion, social status, and even their star sign! However, marriages between couples with different backgrounds are becoming more common today.

Above: Many Indian women, including brides, wear **henna** decorations on their hands.

Education

Each state in India has its own system of courses and examinations. The government provides free primary education for all children up to the fifth grade. In some areas, high-school education is free, too.

Children attend at least ten years of primary and secondary school. A university degree normally takes about three to five years.

Above: Children recite prayers before the start of the school day.

Higher Education

Although early education is free, not all children, especially those in rural areas, go to school. Some leave school at a young age to work. At the end of high school, only those with money or excellent academic achievements can go to college. Indian universities have very high standards, and graduates in fields such as medicine are well received throughout the world.

Below: Students face high standards and very tough competition at Indian universities.

Religion

There are five major religions in India — Hinduism, Islam, Christianity, Buddhism, and Judaism.

About 80 percent of the Indian population practices Hinduism, one of the oldest religions in the world. Hindus worship many gods and goddesses. They study religious texts featuring legends that explain the moral standards they need to follow.

Left: Some Hindus visit the temple to pray and worship every day.

Arab traders brought Islam to India in the tenth century. Today, Muslims make up about one-tenth of the Indian population — the largest religious minority in India. Muslims pray five times a day and fast during Ramadan, the ninth month of the Muslim calendar.

Other religious groups in India include the Christians, the Sikhs, and the Parsis, the descendants of a group that fled Iran between the eighth and tenth centuries.

Above: Religion plays an important part in the lives of most Indians. These Muslims are praying in a mosque.

Language

Many Languages

Hindi and English are India's official languages. The government also recognizes seventeen state languages, including Bengali, Sanskrit, Tamil, and Urdu. Children study in their state language, as well as in Hindi and English. In addition, more than 1,500 **dialects** are spoken in India.

Left: National newspapers are published in all major Indian languages.

Literature

The earliest works of Indian literature were the *Vedas* (VEE-dahs) — hymns and chants in Sanskrit dating back to 1500 B.C. Later, people started to write down *Puranas* (puh-RA-nahs), or legends about gods and goddesses. These stories were handed down from generation to generation. They helped people understand religious ideas and values.

Above: As well as being a successful poet, Rabindranath Tagore (1861–1941) was a dramatist, artist, and musician.

Writers and Poets

During the sixteenth century, Goswami Tulsidas wrote an **epic** poem called *Ramcharitmanas*. It expressed devotion to the Hindu god Ram. One of the greatest Indian poets was Rabindranath Tagore. He won the Nobel Prize for Literature in 1913. Recently, Indian authors have produced prizewinning works in English, such as Vikram Seth's *A Suitable Boy* and Arundhati Roy's *The God of Small Things*.

Arts

Art is a way of life in India. The country abounds with art forms that portray its rich history. One common artistic theme is *rasa* (RAH-sah), which means "the essence of the joy of life."

India's architectural styles reflect its fascinating history. Centuries ago, the Mughal kings built forts throughout the country.

Left: The Red Fort in Delhi is a major tourist attraction today.

Muslim influence can be seen in the many mosques and tombs built during the twelfth century. The Red Fort in Delhi was built by Mughal king Shah Jahan in the seventeenth century. He also built the magnificent Taj Mahal — one of the most famous buildings in the world — for his wife.

British architecture appeared during the colonial period. Many churches and colleges, as well as Mumbai's Gateway of India, were built during that period.

Above: The Mysore Palace houses a throne made of ivory and gold.

Left: Children
in India learn
to play musical
instruments at
a young age.

Music

India has two distinct styles of music
— Hindustani from the north and
Carnatic from the south. Both styles
are based around *ragas* (RA-gahs), or
tunes made up of a small group of notes
that can be played in any order. Ragas
make Indian music unique.

Indian music uses up to five hundred
musical instruments, including the
tanpura (TAHN-poo-rah) and the *sitar*
(sih-TAHR).

Opposite:
The graceful
Manipuri dance
comes from the
Manipur region in
northeastern India.

Dance

Classical Indian dance falls into two main groups — classical and folk. Classical dance forms are based on gestures and facial expressions. Complicated movements and **intricate** footwork make the dances exciting to watch.

Above:
The dancer's movements and expressions tell a story.

Each region in India has distinct forms of folk dance. These are performed mainly during festivals.

Leisure

In their leisure time, Indians living in cities enjoy watching movies and shopping. The countryside offers fewer opportunities for these types of leisure activities. Instead, villagers usually spend evenings chatting with friends. Storytelling is popular throughout India. Performances can last several hours, and some stories feature puppets.

Below: Children love to play board games and cards.

Film

India produces more films than any other country — about eight hundred movies each year! The Mumbai film industry is nicknamed "Bollywood," a name that suggests comparisons with America's Hollywood. Most Indian films are watched only by Indian audiences. Others, including those made by director Satyajit Ray, entertain moviegoers all over the world.

Above: Brightly painted posters advertise the latest movies outside of theaters.

Sport

Indians are passionate about sports. They enjoy traditional sports, such as kite-flying and *kabaddi* (kuh-BAD-dee). They also enjoy games introduced from other countries, such as cricket and soccer.

Kabaddi is a combination of rugby and wrestling. Players have to hold their breaths and dodge members of the opposite team to score points.

Above: Young Indian cricketers dream of playing for their country.

Cricket is popular throughout India. The national team plays around the world and has a huge following. One player, K. S. Rajitsinhji, played for England, reaching a record-breaking 3,000 runs in 1899. The British also introduced soccer to India. Today, India has three major soccer teams based in the northeastern regions.

India's hugely successful hockey team challenges top players at the Olympic Games.

Left: Indians love playing hockey, and they are good at it, too. The first year Indian players competed in the Olympic Games — 1928 — they won the gold medal.

Festivals

Most Indian festivals are religious events that follow the **lunar** calendar. There is a celebration in India almost every week of the year!

Holi

The Hindu festival of Holi takes place in March. It remembers the legend of Holika. Her brother, the king, hated his son, Prahlad, so much that he asked

Below: On Holi, children smear each other with colored powder and get as messy as possible!

Holika, who supposedly could not be burned, to carry the boy into a bonfire. However, the god Vishnu protected Prahlad, and Holika died instead.

Above: Flowers decorate every home during Onam. The main event of the ten-day festival is a boat race.

Onam

Onam, the main festival of Kerala, takes place in August or September. It celebrates the return of the spirit of King Mahabali to his people.

Food

Indian food is popular all over the world. You have probably tasted some of India's famous dishes, such as curries and lentils.

The Indians place great importance on a balanced diet. Their meals vary according to the changing seasons and the crops available. The two main

Left: A typical Indian meal consists of several small dishes served with rice and bread.

foods are rice and wheat. Spices add flavor to accompanying dishes. A typical Indian meal consists of rice, yogurt, vegetable and meat curries, and breads, such as *chapati* (cha-PAH-tee) or *paratha* (pur-RAH-tha).

Above: *Paan* (PAHN) is the leaf of the betel plant smeared with paste and wrapped around spicy ingredients.

Indians love sweets. *Burfee* (BUHR-fee) is made from milk, nuts, dried fruit, and flavorings. In the summer, people enjoy cooling sherbets and refreshing fruit juices.

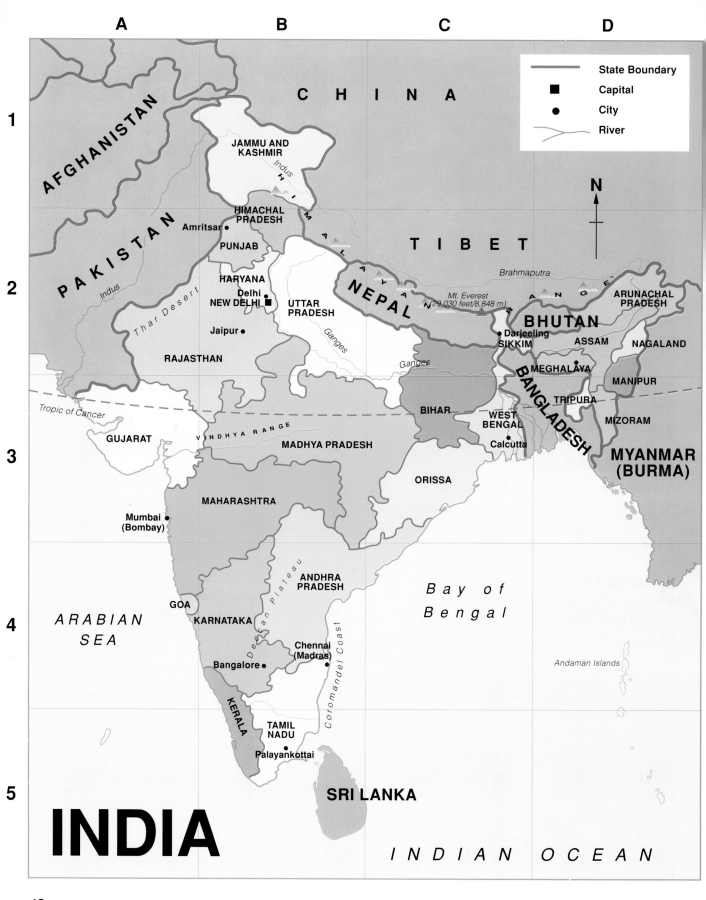

Above: A yogi meditates near a beach.

Afghanistan A1
Amritsar B2
Andaman Islands
   D4
Andhra Pradesh B4
Arabian Sea A4
Arunachal Pradesh
   D2
Assam D2

Bangalore B4
Bangladesh D3
Bay of Bengal C4
Bhutan D2
Bihar C3
Brahmaputra River
   C2

Calcutta C3
Chennai (Madras)
   B4
China B1–C1
Coromandel Coast
   B4

Darjeeling C2

Deccan Plateau B4
Delhi B2

Ganges River B2
Goa A4
Gujarat A3

Haryana B2
Himachal Pradesh B2
Himalayan Range
   B1–D2

Indian Ocean C5–D5
Indus River A2–B2

Jaipur B2
Jammu and Kashmir
   B1

Karnataka B4
Kerala B4–B5

Madhya Pradesh B3
Maharashtra B3
Manipur D3
Meghalaya D2

Mizoram D3
Mt. Everest C2
Mumbai (Bombay)
   A3
Myanmar (Burma)
   D3

Nagaland D2
Nepal B2
New Delhi B2

Orissa C3

Pakistan A2
Palayankottai B5
Punjab B2

Rajasthan A2

Sikkim C2
Sri Lanka B5

Tamil Nadu B5
Thar Desert A2
Tibet C2
Tripura D3
Tropic of Cancer
   A3–D3

Uttar Pradesh B2

Vindhya Range B3

West Bengal C3

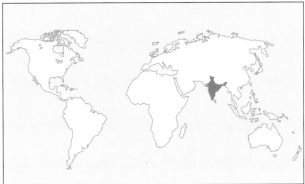

Quick Facts

Official Name	Republic of India
Capital	New Delhi
Official Languages	Hindi and English
Population	936 million (1996/1997 estimate)
Land Area	1.3 million square miles (3.4 million sq. km)
States	Andhra Pradesh, Arunachal Pradesh, Assam, Bihar, Goa, Gujarat, Haryana, Himachal Pradesh, Jammu and Kashmir, Karnataka, Kerala, Madhya Pradesh, Maharashtra, Manipur, Meghalaya, Mizoram, Nagaland, Orissa, Punjab, Rajasthan, Sikkim, Tamil Nadu, Tripura, Uttar Pradesh, West Bengal
Highest Point	Kanchenjunga 28,210 feet (8,598 m)
Major Rivers	Brahmaputra, Ganges, Indus
Important Cities	Bangalore, Calcutta, Chennai, Hyderabad, Mumbai (Bombay), New Delhi
Main Religion	Hinduism (83 percent)
National Animal	Tiger
Currency	Indian rupee (Rs. 43 = U.S. $1 in 1999)

Opposite: The Dudhsagar waterfalls in Goa are the highest in India.

Glossary

archaeologists: scientists who study ancient cultures by analyzing tools, pottery, and other remains.

bindi (BIN-dee)**:** a colored dot worn by Indian women on their foreheads.

burfee (BUHR-fee)**:** a sweet food made of milk, nuts, and dried fruit.

chapati (cha-PAH-tee)**:** a round, flat, soft bread served with rice and curry.

colony: a territory under the control of another nation.

democratic: relating to a system of government in which supreme power rests with the people.

dharma chakra (DHAR-mah CHAK-rah)**:** the wheel of life, a Buddhist symbol that dates back to the second century B.C.

dialects: regional varieties of a certain language.

dynasty: a line of rulers belonging to the same family.

epic: relating to a long poem usually centered around a hero and written in a grand style.

exiled: forced to leave one's country and prohibited from returning.

henna: a reddish-brown plant dye used on skin and hair.

intricate: complex; complicated.

kabaddi (kuh-BAD-dee)**:** a game that combines rugby and wrestling.

landmark: a distinguishing monument.

lunar: relating to the movements of the moon.

mutiny: a rebellion of sailors or soldiers against their officers.

nationalists: people who are devoted and loyal to their country.

overpopulated: having too many people, putting a strain on resources and facilities.

paratha (pur-RAH-tha)**:** round, fried bread, sometimes cooked with egg or filled with vegetables or meat.

sari: a woman's garment worn wrapped around the body.

sitar (sih-TAHR)**:** a stringed musical instrument with a pear-shaped body and a long neck.

strikes: (n) protests.

tanpura (TAHN-poo-rah)**:** a four-stringed musical instrument.

More Books to Read

The Adventures of Young Krishna.
   Diksha Dalal-Clayton
   (Oxford University)

*India. Country Insights, City and Village
   Life* series. David Cumming
   (Raintree/Steck Vaughn)

India. Festivals of the World series.
   Falaq Kadga (Gareth Stevens)

India. Games People Play series. Dale
   E. Howard (Children's Press)

*The Indian Subcontinent. Places and
   People* series. Anita Ganeri
   (Franklin Watts)

Sacred River. Ted Lewin
   (Clarion Books)

*Science in Ancient India. Science of the
   Past* series. Melissa Stewart
   (Franklin Watts)

Sikhism. Discovering Religions series.
   Sue Penney (Raintree/
   Steck Vaughn)

The Taj Mahal. Great Buildings series.
   Christine Moorcroft (Raintree/
   Steck Vaughn)

Videos

*In the Wild: The Elephants of India with
   Goldie Hawn.* (PBS)

Music of India. (Hollywood
   Select Video)

Wild India. (Discovery Communication)

Windows to the World: India.
   (Ivn Entertainment)

Web Sites

theory.tifr.res.in/bombay/history/
   index.html

www.angelfire.com/in/myindia/
   tajmahal.html

cgi.pathfinder.com/time/time100/
   leaders/profile/ghandi.html

www.aboutindia.com/

Due to the dynamic nature of the Internet, some web sites stay current longer than
others. To find additional web sites, use a reliable search engine with one or more
of the following keywords to help you locate information on India: *Bollywood,
Gandhi, Ganges, Hinduism, Mumbai, New Delhi, Red Fort, Shah Jahan, Taj Mahal.*

Index